THE
WILDERNESS

THE
WILDERNESS

POEMS

SANDRA
LIM

W. W. Norton & Company   New York   London

First Edition

For information about permission to reproduce selections from this book,
write to Permissions, W. W. Norton & Company, Inc.,
500 Fifth Avenue, New York, NY 10110

For information about special discounts for bulk purchases, please contact
W. W. Norton Special Sales at specialsales@wwnorton.com or 800-233-4830

Production manager: Louise Parasmo

Library of Congress Cataloging-in-Publication Data

Lim, Sandra.
[Poems. Selections]
The wilderness : poems / Sandra Lim. — First edition.
pages cm
ISBN 978-0-393-34957-3 (pbk.)
I. Title.
PS3612.I467A6 2014
811'.6—dc23

2014011420

W. W. Norton & Company, Inc. 500 Fifth Avenue, New York, N.Y. 10110
www.wwnorton.com

W. W. Norton & Company Ltd., Castle House, 75/76 Wells Street, London W1T 3QT

CONTENTS

1

SMALL CONTAINER, FURY   15

SNOWDROPS   16

HUMAN INTEREST STORY   17

AMOR FATI   19

THE VANISHING WORLD   21

NATURE MORTE   22

WILDLIFE   24

ABOVE US ARE THE LAST LIGHTS   25

WINTERING   26

2

VER NOVUM   29

RITE OF SPRING   39

ENVOI: LAZARUS   41

3

THE NEW WORLD   45

CERTAINTY   46

SELVA ANTICA   48

GARDEN QUARREL   49
1. THE CHANGE   49
2. REASON IS BUT CHOOSING   50
3. SNAKE   52

CERTAINTY   53

FALL   55

CHEVAL SOMBRE   56

ENVOI: ORPHEUS   58

THE CONCERT   59

HYPERBALLAD   62

UNFLEUR   63

4

HOMAGE TO MISTRESS BRADSTREET   67
1. INVOCATION   67
2. NOW, VOYAGER   68
3. WINTER DIPTYCH   70
4. BRIDE'S DESSERT   72
5. CONVERSION NARRATIVE   73
6. SÉANCE   74
7. POETRY (THE AUTHOR TO HER BOOK)   76
8. MY LIPS CLOSED OVER THE WORLD THAT
   BROKE THROUGH   77
9. BLACK PAINTING   78

AT THE OTHER END OF A WIRE   79

VOUS ET NUL AUTRE   80

REMARKS ON MY SCULPTURE   85

AUBADE   86

EARTHQUAKE WEATHER   88

THE DARK WORLD   89

CLIFFS   91

NOTES   93

ACKNOWLEDGMENTS   95

The world was like a faraway planet to which
I could never return. I thought what a fine place it was, full of
things that people can look into and enjoy.
—HOLLY (SISSY SPACEK), *BADLANDS*

Pioneering is not feeling well.
—JOHN BERRYMAN, *HOMAGE TO MISTRESS BRADSTREET*

The greater the spirit, the greater the beast.
—JEWISH-DUTCH PROVERB

1

SMALL CONTAINER, FURY

Rembrandt paints his carcass of beef.

You see a little blood near the poppies
and don't think of detachment.

Humbert and his girl are driving across America.

One has a thirst so unslakeable, one walks
right into the river.

How exciting spring is! and how errant,

holding out love and death
like a platter of the daintiest cakes.

As I do my work, I think, let me topple,
wear thin. Let the world eat me, but

then, let the world sob, not me.

Spring comes forward as a late-winter confection, and I cannot decide if it advances a philosophy of meekness or daring.

This year's snowdrops: is it that they are spare, and have a slightly fraught lucidity, or are they proof that pain, too, can be ornate?

Even a propped skull is human nature. And its humor is monstrous, rich with an existence that owes nothing to anyone.

Fat little pearls against the ice, battering softly, try even fewer qualities—

To say that you love someone or something *to death* is to hover around the draw of irrevocability.

More faith is asked of us, a trained imagination against the ice-white.

Snow would have been breaking the drifts that day, on a mild
mood.

My father was boarding at the home of a missionary couple in
Seoul, getting by on books and the radio and cheap noodles.

His older brother hanged himself that winter in Pusan. They
would say afterward that it was a plain death, funded by bad
numbers, some selfishness, unusual cold.

Think of a needle dropped into the sea.

He had a pleasantly objective feeling about himself that morning,
as the early sky gently ripped into red. He thought about Business
English, the truth of money.

Across town, a diary opened. And there were the white, cooling
coals in barrels.

There was a pretty young wife and one serious boy and one very
quiet girl. They awakened one day to a new planet, where the
spaces between people appeared slightly widened.

Maybe you can't penetrate events with reportage, but facts have a
sly, unanswerable texture that appears social.

To relieve ourselves of open-ended narrative, we read into the winter stars all evening. There are just stars and stars and stars.

We know what it's like to fall in love and be disassembled, but we still want to pull death right off the bodies of one another.

These were spectacular nights, said my father. They were full of philosophy and political theory, noisy reversals, French movies.

The romantic grace we comprehend sits with ease in the real world; it is almost nothing.

Now he is carrion, stitched forever in the cramp of a trial.

No one can evict us from books! he used to say, running through astonishment at full speed.

AMOR FATI

Inside every world there is another world trying to get out,
and there is something in you that would like to discount this
    world.

The stars could rise in darkness over heartbreaking coasts,
and you would not know if you were ruining your life or
    beginning a real one.

You could claim professional fondness for the world around you;
the pictures would dissolve under the paint coming alive,

and you would only feel a phantom skip of the heart, absorbed so
    in the colors.
Your disbelief is a later novel emerging in the long, long shadow of
    an earlier one—

is this the great world, which is whatever is the case?
The sustained helplessness you feel in the long emptiness of days is
    matched

by the new suspiciousness and wrath you wake to each morning.
Isn't this a relationship with your death, too, to fall in love with
    your inscrutable life?

Your teeth fill with cavities. There is always unearned happiness
  for some,
and the criminal feeling of solitude. Always, everyone lies about
  his life.

THE VANISHING WORLD

It's said that people tend to believe God believes what they believe.

When I was young I loved to get up before every dawn of the world, still sweetly baffled by the possibility of unbelief.

Perhaps grace is not so poor a thing that it can't also appear in this instance like a new definition of luck,

akin to tiny blossoms out of cactus thorns in spring, their loneliness crushing your lungs.

Isn't everything sloughed from the same star? What is believable and possible, what is acceptable and what is nothing?

Caught between the old and new year, why do you think that the old will be famous for its pain, the new from the liberation from pain?

Some kind of belief still runs off me in strings;

to enjoy the clarifying effect of participation without remainder may be the most mysterious thing.

When I come to the right place, I believe I'll paint a door on it and walk right through.

NATURE MORTE

You are given two things today, one is an angry nail in your side;
Changing what you are able to sense is the second thing you are
  gifted.

Nature is always a referred existence, writes Emerson, never a
  presence.
Who knows where the time goes, sings Sandy Denny. Who can
  bear to hear it?

One reaches the moment when one loses words—in the pastoral,
  in the cosmic?
Think about the scars on the planets, & how patient those stars
  seem to be.

I am painting the natural landscape with my eyes closed today. It
  is like writing
A poem with all the cross-outs left in; an expression like *never
  thought I'd see the day.*

Nature that begins with unknowable & ends with more
  monotonous hills.
Today, I want to be the country-fried philosophe or a Hudson
  River School painting.

When this life is over, describe to me how its concave & convex
forms are & are not.

We live amid surfaces, writes Emerson, & the true art of life is to
skate well on them.

WILDLIFE

I can see draughty stars drift
inside my skull.

Roots and boles and boughs and leaves
press at the backs of my eyes.

A spider rambles inside my body and
scuttles out of my mouth.

This suit is an agony.

Black flies from the creek fall into my teacup—
keep one eye on the world, they say.

ABOVE US ARE THE LAST LIGHTS

planting something within us
that also represents death for the
taking at every turn;

greeting the season
all coated in soft silver
with a strong handshake;

loving and hating,
those buttons done up all the way
to the top of your sweater.

WINTERING

The stars gave up their deep drifting and touched bottom.

No clouds toppled across the snow wilderness.

No gloom-dark tree-glitter winding and twining its silks.

Blankness, egg-quiet.

The level sprawl of the world drew away tinily, in every direction.

Afternoons remained unknown to each other.

Yet loss keeps thudding past my house, telling me I'm not done.

My hearts, still leaping like rats.

2

VER NOVUM

First day of spring—
it's maintaining, calling, shining.
Probably it hurts its business a little.

/

She sings in response:

What strokes my abdomen, titillates my fur?
My coils sweeten, all tensed and set.

The season is a burst harp.

/

Soirs, evenings. And yet it has some afternoon in it as well.
I don't need much more than this to fall in love.

/

Reading deeply had incarnadined her cheeks.

/

Maytime! My mint going out of its mind,
my garlic groaning quietly.
I feel like a complete change of circumstances.

/

This time of year challenges you
like a little magician

fanning the day's cards
brusquely in your face.

Pick a card, any card.
Change the flesh into word.

That word may sound broken into:
you can hear life beating

on its fiery way within it, brutalities
and banalities going about their custom.

/

It was like an oar going into water, gliding.

You could hear the clatter of the stars
coming out, like falling stones

in spring rain, remote from theology.

/

She sits down to dinner
in a casual trattoria,

surrounded by Dionysian big cats,
her racy expat friends.

She sets down a brisk narrative of her life
in loony detail and Taurean pleasure.

She used to sit and cry, thinking about it,
loving it no less.

The spectacle is not discouraging!
The way she beholds it has the sin of pride.

/

April and March, overcurious about sex,
thump against the screen door.

Lovelessness in these months
seems a travesty,

like wigs in sherbet colors, too loud against
the season's paradisal light.

/

Snowdrops looking tatty.
They don't feel the threat
that I would feel.

/

Investigating his wish to die,
he goes to a teaching hospital.

The puppet feels the hand at times,
wildflowers, their underneath.

/

The season lays palely
on a white platter,

its calm faded eye looks
far beyond us.

We sense our own claims
shrinking.

/

For fear of the winter's teeth,
the spring queen had them pulled.
Now it cannot chew,

it must subsist on slop.
Now its face has no mouth,
and its hair never saw scissors.

The queen folds her mind over it,
as if discovering a new crystal.

/

If word can become flesh,
now leaning its forehead against cool glass,

now discovering a passion
for Thomas Hardy,

can't it be the spur that coaxes
out the strangest beast

within the beast, the spirit?

/

The cat in heat is
in the grip of a new idea:
she barks!

/

The sense of the season is pursued through
its reprimands: crocuses and pansies,

snowdrop, scilla, a Tête-à-Tête
daffodil. Tulips, peonies,

azaleas, and hyacinths.
Jack-in-the-pulpit.

/

Affection chains thy tender days.
Candles burning into their tins.

/

In the spring the quinces

/

Like a water-flower dropped
in a glass of water,
spring grows—

/

at times meaning
the world, its fan of pages;
other times, only conscious

of something turning.

/

The grip of solitude—

/

All my wet trees, breathing happily

/

From half-dark to half-dark,
I read autumn poems in spring.

Buson writes about stepping
on his dead wife's comb
in their dark bedroom.

In fact, she outlived him by thirty-one years.

The chill from that comb, and the snap
of eros and solitude and imagining,
all in flower.

/

Threes conclude into ones,
as in the Christian mysteries.
Grief brought to numbers cannot be so fierce.

/

What is the heart of the problem?

The flaring March lily subverts
all our emotional gourmandizing,

like a serene, inviolable erotomane
cupping its ear to listen to our true secrets.

/

The explorer with his walleye
and fading map peers into the distance.

He is so far from where he started,
and wasn't this the point?

To have the cookbook turn
into parable, or vice versa,

it didn't matter. Now, it was as if
he were a new pair of scissors

biting into a clean sheet of paper.
Rupture, instead of continuity.

He wills his eyeball into place
and walks boldly into the conditions.

/

The heart's best trick?
For the one and only spring you will be given this year,
let your happiness crawl all over the floors.

/

Spate of thundershowers in spring.
It has an intellectual appeal,
pointing to nothing.

/

Now the coldness merely asks you
to tear your life apart
and begin again.

Pilgrim, throw it away, make it larger.

/

Spring, which says it's never been unfaithful,
mixing insult and provocation.

RITE OF SPRING

Dimmed summer. The fortune-teller reads
my palm in the humid dark.

That spring I could not be whole.

Feeling atonal and unconciliatory,
I went to see *The Rite of Spring.*

I went to see what art in general is about
and what people are really like.

I wanted to watch the shape
of a movement,
the trajectory of a body as it makes

the shapes that it will in a limited ambit,
revolving around an implied center.

The young virgin dances herself to death
to bring forth
the flowering of spring.

Free-verse rhythms,
ritualized, vivid decisions of actions.

I went to see what people are really like
in a thousand human ways.

All these gestures from life, deformed
to suit a more open, imagined music.

She won't make an affirmation
or a negation of my destiny,

but it's good for business, the way she eats
through the score of a life and keeps me
hypnotized by the future destination.

I watch the fortune-teller as I watch
an absorbing movie:
I just want to know what happens.

ENVOI: LAZARUS

Lazarus woke to the miracle of no longer fearing failure.
He lifted his two sides from the ground as he tried
To speak, one part gathering darkness, one part humming.
When he walked out, he glimpsed a world never tried.
At the crucial point, there is yet more than one way
Of proceeding, but it seldom appears that way.

3

The world we see never is the world that is: the senseless morning
light cuts its white eyes open.

What is the lecture of the darkest pines, the way they hang their
stillness against us?

If I beggar myself for love, do I move from night into more night?

If I swallow a mouthful of ground glass, do I not slip past
languages?

Thunderous wakefulness is ceaseless needles through the casing.

There are only the living and the dead: roses climbing a battered
trellis. A caterpillar turns its hard black goggles upon the cold
meat of me.

Drinking wholly from the world remains dark argument, hardly
moral.

To be living in the feast sweetens my idea of death, its
foreknowledge and its art.

Affliction, make yourself a scar upon my house and count the
ways.

Edward Taylor was a frontier minister who wrote a prolific amount of devotional poetry. The poems are full of deep piety, learned and quiet, but sometimes an errant wildness runs under the seams of his words.

It's said that he wrote poetic meditations to put himself in the correct spiritual state for his communion with Christ.

I imagine the task swallowing him each time, moving its own patient way like snowmelt. A poem may hold the unwieldy pieces of the earth together with a whole heart; a poem may cut that heart to lace.

His first wife, Elizabeth Fitch, bore eight children; five died in infancy. Taylor wrote more and more sermons and poems.

Sometimes a conceit makes itself necessary in the safety of the impasse between word and world. *And make my Soule thy holy Spoole to bee,* writes Taylor.

His parishioners were called to worship in the wilderness with a beat of a drum, amid cold plants, the night coming on, undelivered ashes of stars.

Flocks take to the sky at dusk. I have wondered if the parishioners counted the days.

As in: Did they ever travel past the corrective of the afterworld to stand in the strong spine of rivers? According to Taylor: *In Heaven soaring up, I dropt an Eare On Earth: and oh! sweet Melody!*

—(Or weren't there deranged cries in the wilderness, too?)

Taylor's trust appears both adamantine and vulnerable, like the slow plan of the flowering grass or torn, stilled clouds.

Alone in his study, he writes down some dimensions—
I'm but a Flesh and Blood bag, Oh!

Consider the strange and riotous interior, through which so many nameless things fly.

As weeds continue to idle their tails, leaves molder right on time. In the rafters of the sky, a pristine star shines with unassailability. It can't be taught a thing.

The wilderness: I cannot get around the back of it.

SELVA ANTICA

What dreams! Those forests!
—SAMUEL BECKETT, *ENDGAME*

It was a way to think
in the unearthly openness of time.

You stepped away from this world
so that you could consider it from afar.

Did the moon still appear cold and indifferent?
Did a human sound seem singular?

You only remember that there was nothing
to eat in this wilderness,

so that by the time spring came, in generation and decay,
it was not abstract enough for you—

In your want you conjured more blankness,
a prodigious emptiness, *the fair schoolroom*

of the sky. Paradise would be paper-white,
a way to ease into this nothingness.

GARDEN QUARREL

1. The Change

There was something theatrical in the air,
like the coming of a circus.

I don't know, the world seemed a dummy run
after that dawn-cold snake.

I realized life could be
like the nest of some tremendous bird.

I was always a religious bitch,
all prolepsis and superstition.

2. Reason Is But Choosing

Eve ate the apple
she tasted the snake

Adam ate Eve
he tasted the apple

Their hunger
had the grandeur
of a famine

A *tristesse*
falls upon the scene
like a light rainfall

There is something mysterious
about lyric poetry

The long glare walls
of evening
were constructed in a spirit of play

Adam's a *tragédien*
Eve opens and closes her legs like a book
No one is waiting for life to begin

Their tears eventually
turn back into
the leaves of the tree

3. Snake

The snake says it needs a tree, so here is a tree.
It says, make the tree stir its tops and play
their emerald lights. I do. I slide the clouds
off the sun for good measure.

Two nights it has lain in wait, this figure with no arms.
Now it approaches the shimmering lights in the tree,
studies the glassy dullness of the couple.
They don't know yet that they are alive.

The snake tells her to take her thumb out of
her mouth; a soul needs the presence
of desire. It says it's worth dying to understand
the conditions under which figure, tree, man,

or woman might smash. She moves toward
the moral impunity of the apple. I ease it from its branch,
so that it is snake-low. She eats it carefully,
inspecting the potential of the snake with each bite.

CERTAINTY

Perhaps you can tell children that the world is always a more
beautiful place than you can suppose,

and then you release them into their future, the black row of trees
in the distance.

She died suddenly in midwinter, in the same bed in which her
husband died years earlier; it still sagged on his side. Her second
husband remained in Japan with his first family.

She used to say, what my three girls do when they are on their own
is unimaginable to me.

My mother is the middle daughter, a garden of inaudible tunes.
The four of them lived in a mean house in Seoul.

One yellowing picture of my grandmother remains, and her face
turns away from the camera, as the rabbit senses the hound;

she was said to be a solitary eater, an inner thing. What did she
promise the world that she wasn't able to make good on?

A child who abruptly feels the frontiers of experience assert
themselves in her: at the funeral my mother cries so hard she can't
feel her hands for days,

it explains how she scratches herself raw, meaningless.

You have always believed these are your themes: fate, the negative pleasures of dipping oneself in acid.

You think it will rescue you from your simplicity, remarks my mother from the doorway, but art is never the ace in the hole.

I am not a stupid child. I am not even a child any longer, with her hesitant, then terrible certainty, that loss is tragic, not only pointless.

When she is lonely, my mother cooks; and when she is happy, she knows to hide it.

FALL

Each night, the same dream: I'm an odd Victorian mansion
in a field of wheat. And I'm either waiting for the field
to catch fire or the hearse of love to pull up to the manse.
Don't wake me. In daylight, my mother talks of brideliness
as a measure of time: in a kind of flower, a narrative of ascension.
I intimate some sort of border is being discussed,
but I can't concentrate for the sake of all the beautiful things
claiming my attentions in the tawny fields.
There, a blankness without meanness, such as one finds
in a naked sea with all its fundamental majesty.

From time to time, I like to learn a severe truth about a familiar
    deception: a beautiful watch lying new in its case.

A precise, coruscating luxury,

The future arrives under the sign of its own negation.

A curious traversal of tenses, *le dernier cri,* and so

The hope of even seeing you again is slipping.

I'm so shaken, I act calmly for the rest of the afternoon:

At last I shall see my hunger for meaning go free.

The world could be like a faraway planet to which I declare,

Free at last: I shall see my hunger for meaning go.

I'm so shaken, I act calmly for the rest of the afternoon;

The hope of even seeing you again is slipping.

A curious traversal of tenses, *le dernier cri,* and so

The future arrives under the sign of its own negation.

A precise, coruscating luxury:

A beautiful watch lying new in its case. I like to learn a familiar
truth about a severe deception from time to time.

ENVOI: ORPHEUS

I say the look back
was coldness mixed with longing.

Afterward,
he could finally think.

Many have imagined
what the song must have sounded like:

Not language breaking.
Not how safe it is to be gone.

But the world
seeping in so quickly.

For a moment,
world arranges itself around artist.

The wine of annihilation rises within
him, a new acuteness.

Elsewhere, a disappointed lover mutilates
another tree with the departed's initials,

restored to disinterested making.

THE CONCERT

My best friend says I wake up in the morning
and rage.

—Do I? I ask her, incredulous.
I see myself as a mild, hemmed-in sort of person.

—You rage, she says. You rage against:

    a. a.m. snow
    b. the dilemma of the soul
    c. your fate
    d. all varieties of longing

And here I have always wanted to be as cold and ferocious as a
    star.

But if I rage, let me make my voice its capacious forest.
Let it be the melancholy that comedy is meant to overcome!

/

Portnoy says that underneath their skirts girls all have cunts.

There's mine,
cheerful, *au fond*, in its ineffable femininity.

It lights my privacy,
endorses
the faintly guilty air of my naturalness.

The unenactable idea is that we all have souls.

Next to a soul,
the body's curious reticence obtains.

I can wag my lower self gladder and gladder,
but my soul, it wants
to stay up, write through the night.

If you press the hollow of my throat, my soul pulls a face.

/

in the hour, the music, of a.m. snow,
in the constellation of sleep, anti-sleep, and the wintry mix—
the sweet council of snow's philosophical flights.

longing is a spine. in the erotic rustle of maroon Victoriana. in a
hunger so unappeasable, one becomes a criminal. not a snore in a
rose all morning.

the slightly withheld motion of yearning makes it look dragged by
   destiny.

/

—Errancy, I will say to her later, might be the silvery bloom on
   me.
Let it be the comedy that melancholy equably praises.

Let me be like a mouse in an enormous cheese
excited by how much cheese there is to eat.

I think my interior, it must be a killing machine,
I ask it what the shooting means, I am trying to think.
I let it look right through me, having no choice in the matter,
its no-space and its no-time, they bring me to my knees.
It straps me to my body, as if I were made for it,
it begins its waste with a slight forward pull.
I help it with its loneliness, but I avert my eyes;
I know that it will always be a good part of me.
As it continues its arrivals, I will not say I'm shot,
as it burns all over, I'll know I'm not erased.
They say with mystery, all things are possible,
somewhere in the huge whisper of the coldest oceans.
Sweet water brims through the winter ices. O philosopher
of destructions, nevertheless my heart is pounding—

UNFLEUR

Spring obliges
my imagination
of return

then
it annihilates it

What is death
but reason
in flawless submission
to itself

No
not reason

something stonier

4

HOMAGE TO MISTRESS BRADSTREET

1. Invocation

Coolness sails down from the moon in the wilderness:

> in this landscape,
> > the erotica of being made free.

> But it makes me think of a chair and a book and a bed
with a lamp near it.

> Desire is to go away from a star.

So let me consider it from here, from inside the head of my demon.

2. *Now, Voyager*

I first thought her a pure fury,
or Last Blues. Or everything in the wide world
that was cold, inscrutable, and beastly.

Sometimes she was innocent of metaphor,
just a girl disappearing with the phone into a closet.
Other times she would lead me to the edge

of my human being, where the meaning would be
seeping away, and say with a flourish, *Not yet enjoyed!*
And it was a relief to be someone so angry,

to put across the distortions without and within.
A journey like this appears to hold out the promise
of a rescue, an immense life in the formlessness.

So we come to stand on the deck of an agèd ocean liner.
The sea hoards nothing, our senses are alive and bright.
The captain says we are opening into a territory

of raw wishes and the "merely" beautiful,
past heartbreak, transcendence, past return.
How could this territory have anything to do with us?

There is something exciting about it, nevertheless.
Something mistaken and wholly familiar,
hatchet-minded, and eager with beginning.

3. Winter Diptych

I.

All my life I have gone to church
with a kind of persistence.

I wanted one work of mine
to be as fresh as this world and more

spacious than my consideration of it.
I was not out to burn up

my life for a mystery;
my daily experience was acknowledged

in my belief, in its reticence.
Its reserve exceeds me in every way.

II.

When at the end of all pioneering,
I will think, how glad He will be
to hear how his pupils' memories
accord with his own.

But it was only the first winter,
and in truth I was dreaming of
the home I'd just left and of when
father's library would arrive here.

4. *Bride's Dessert*

A form of counsel

1. Peel 4–6 oranges. Slice into very thin rounds.

2. Arrange onto plate (a glass one is traditional).

3. Sprinkle with bourbon or brandy and let sit in the refrigerator
   for 2 hours. The important thing is to get the oranges very cold.

4. Before serving, sprinkle with a little shredded coconut and
   garnish with a maraschino cherry, and/or violets.

Serves 4.

Also called "Orange Ambrosia."

5. *Conversion Narrative*

What I was trying to tell you about my burning house—

Now ~~that I am dead~~, I can tell you.

It is only as nothing that the soul
can be larger than what I imagine.

When she saw the house on fire
my youngest daughter said,

When I grow up, I want to be lightning.

Suffering must have quite a different dimension
from what I have experienced so far.

The weight of flame in our faces
increased the parade ground of our mystery.

It said the surprise is on its way.

6. Séance

I had time and liberty enough
     to propose a great many things to myself;

             and now you raise me up again,
     to show you a public belief
               realized in private,
           an idea of art and of mortal life

          In the mornings the Lord did say, Get up and be birdlike
and I would consent once more
     to live within this peculiar dream

              —my soul correcting by inches, holding itself out
                 to the world that will not quite hold it—

     and even in my sleep, I would keep track of the time,
though you see, the world was always saying to die, actually—

Discovering my privacy was like coming upon blindness—

I clean the blackened oven,
I tend my garden, I read, I teach the children
parables, they draw pictures

It is not a small life

I am not haunted
by nature, not even by the vast stretches of silence in it,
something else is melting
the days:

thawing them to a dazzling supernatural—
there, human nature is flowering,
is saying to think more coldly

bewilderment free on the surface of such an expanse

—these baby birds stunned by
their wings,
now they can see clouds not in any book

7. Poetry (The Author to Her Book)

It's the thing I choose,
a nice bed in the hospital
from which to write about
spring snow on the forest floor.

8. My Lips Closed Over the World That Broke Through

I was a small seed, bare as a soul.

I often mistook my hands for hooks.

I sung high and thunderous and scared at the revival meetings.

I would look at the sky and think of a tin punch lantern.

In the evenings, one side of me would often get even with the
    other.

This is my life! cries the wild doll, *and I'm the judge.*

If you wake up in a conflagration of hunger, eat up the black fact
    of it.

9. *Black Painting*

The night always knows when to complete itself:

    just before dawn.
        The sun will never know its ambitious secrets.

Though left so long and so far from light in this wild place,
    the night becomes strange. Its aesthetic satisfactions

        may insufficiently repay
            the wind blowing through
  a little soul—

mortality a frontier in the arc of it,
    waiting to see how we solved being alive.

    O night! In this lunacy, we could be so happy together,

  thinking about thinking about
        the sun's brightest provocations.

AT THE OTHER END OF A WIRE

When he called, there were 261 emotions
at play. I thought there were only wistfulness,
humiliation, and mere bitterness left, but lo,
I see now the brilliance in the numbers.
Emotions 75 and 78 made me happy just to know
they existed. I felt less alone, more impervious.
I was emboldened by the existence of 152.
Though, how was I supposed to accept 9, 14, and 179?
We deserved better, distress and indigence aside.
Something about 260 broke the spell inside me
and offered up a tiny shift: I opened my eyes in the fog
and tore off the surfaces of 261 and 4 with a great shout.

VOUS ET NUL AUTRE

I have hung our dwelling with enormous
nets, crackerjack feeler though you are.

But nets don't help us in the awful
enormity of the emotion of thinking.

The electrifying interiors keep
turning their faces from the light.

/

The moon's passionate disinterest.
Stage blood.
Contrails overhead.

The dynamic properties of will
elude us.
Feeling is clawing out of her hair.

/

Thinking through the feeling, yet

the body won't comment on this event,
refuses to draw a moral from itself.

Won't it at least reveal the
dramatic force of a last stand?

Is it just being fiercely economical:
a broken heart as dreamy suspension,

as glinting aporia. A lecture on the weather.

/

A boat as swan as burning nettles:
such feelings.

/

Instead of sweet thoughtlessness, I could
taste my mind churning.

It was a great relief that my thoughts
had taken over feeling about our sorrows.

I wanted to turn over all my wildness to them,
so that they could harbor it in English-language sounds.

/

A stunned heart uses up whole days.

You appeared crucial,
not only interesting.

Feelings escaping out from the
willful I, the one that wants always

to place its unthinkable petals on high branches.

/

Or: you were in a conflagration
and lived.

Just living what you were feeling,
empty enough.

Let the fans of panic and longing whirr.
Do not desire me when I'm unable to burn.

/

The coffee all boiled out in the kitchen.
The birds dead at the bottoms of their cages.

When the spring slips the yoke of winter as if
out from under the sway of a particular monarch,

will we feel the second thought of a hovering,
that sensation of lushness, again?

/

I will lose sight of you. Still, in fluted, blued departure,
the cold spray of fear.

Feelings held together now by malicious ideas
and missing their true meanings.

/

Before he goes and she helps
herself with plans, prior to the seamed
self saying, *let them, let them wreck in me*—

They are so sorry for each other's anger.
Nevertheless, they rummage inside
themselves for their tiny knives of feeling

/

and all they want now is relief,
not from feeling but from the anticipation
of an answer, for all the formal difference in between.

/

But feelings keep opening their myriad dark
flowers for you, their thousand petals of thought.

REMARKS ON MY SCULPTURE

In 1973, I found myself engaged in a sort of assemblage
of odd pieces of organic material, connected in a series.
I asked the questions, what is a subject?
What are the isolations around what something is?
The shapes and dimensions of my figures, its volumes
of air and light and dew, had a fraught and transient quality.
I used string and wire, the scent of snow and winter dawn,
fanaticism. I hated less than the wholeness of a situation.
Hunger is a conventional metaphor for desire, and here
I use it simply—it is just what the hand does, where the
eye leads. The absent senses of a word on a starless night,
implied and precluded, mediate the tone of a condition.
Not instances of a geometry or some other larger order;
more or less thinkable, it is paid for by existence.

AUBADE

From the last stars to sunrise the world is dark and enduring
and emptiness has its place.

Then, to wake each day to the world's unwavering
limits, you have to think about passion differently, again.

Don't we forgive everything of a lover
if we are the motive,
if love promises to take us to many places, to even larger themes?

Faithlessness is a heart glancing down
a plumed avenue
in which one is serenaded by myriad, scattering birds.

Thunder in the air begins opening appetites;
everyone is being true to themselves, they think—

And then it is having your right arm sheared off,
and the whole world gets to touch you, chime your losses.

I turn to my imagination, but its eyes are still
green, as if from
too much looking on at equatorial gardens.

Still, if I were you I would linger here,
deepen in the rottenness,
learn something about the world, about the desire for safety.

Then, I'd make an instrument from the ruins,
something awfully beautiful.

I would sit down to eat as if I were reading a poem.
I would observe how the night
went into the day with a special grandeur.

It could be like swallowing a sword and growing surprised
by how good it is, how it opens.

And then maybe to sing out with a throat like that—
saying look,
look how the world has touched me.

EARTHQUAKE WEATHER

Art is not the lie
that tells the truth.

Sometimes it calls me
later than usual to say less.

Earthquakes originate
well out of the reach
of real weather.

When your fear of them
turns
to desire,

at least
conceal your excitement,

so that I can think about
new feelings
and new problems

in relative peace, apart from
cause and effect.

THE DARK WORLD

Pierre looks out the prison window and laughs and laughs,
because the world is inside him.

I'm terrified because I love the world but which one.

It snows all afternoon, but in the west, the canyons are cooling in
the shifting natural light.

Each world curls at its edges, and yet I am ever biddable in either
direction.

Here is the interior holding up its torn roots in front of your eyes,
seigneurial and glittering.

I taste it slowly, the afternoon being as wide as a death. I hear the
wind and the snow in the wind.

I'm half open and half shut—

dragging the chains of the day through the fat blood of a life,
listening to the mathematics of one season drifting over to
another.

I want bars again, restaurants that stay open late, gossip in the kitchen; the bright tessellations of painful wishing, movies, plumes of envy, flower stalls.

Let me stay awake, as whole worlds keep arriving with raggedness, with their synoptic force.

CLIFFS

Words are afraid up here.

The rapture and the terrifying exposure.

Strange birds roosting, a human voice shouting a world's-end
   shout.

Snow hurries to the meeting, wanting to cover the waking in my
   body.

I could fill up the sea with this waking.

The outlook is thrilling; it satisfies.

It goes even further than the view from the heights of love.

It eats the roof off the sky.

NOTES

"Ver Novum" borrows "Affection chains thy tender days" from William Shakespeare's *The Two Gentlemen of Verona*. "Grief brought to numbers cannot be so fierce" is from John Donne's "The Triple Fool."

"Selva Antica" borrows the line "the fair schoolroom of the sky" from Emily Dickinson's poem that begins "I shall know why— when Time is over," from R. W. Franklin's #215 variorium edition of 1998.

"The Concert" borrows its final two lines from a Czesław Miłosz interview in *The Paris Review*, "The Art of Poetry. No. 70."

"Remarks on My Sculpture" borrows its title and first line from artist Fred Sandback's statement, "Remarks on My Sculpture, 1966–86."

ACKNOWLEDGMENTS

My deepest gratitude to Louise Glück for her generosity, wit, and guidance.

Grateful acknowledgment is given to the editors of the following publications in which these poems first appeared, sometimes in different versions: *Boston Review*: "Amor Fati." *Columbia Poetry Review*: "Now, Voyager." *Drunken Boat*: "Vous et Nul Autre." *Guernica/A Magazine of Art & Politics*: "Envoi: Lazarus." *Literary Imagination*: "Certainty." *Martha's Vineyard Arts & Ideas*: "Above Us Are the Last Lights." *Memorious*: "Fall" and "Remarks on My Sculpture." *Omnidawn*: "Cliffs." *The Volta*: "Unfleur."

Special thanks to Katie Peterson and James Shea for their careful attention to this collection and for their abiding support. Thanks to David Adjmi, Kate Isard, and Lisa Fishman for sustaining me in different ways throughout the writing of this book. I also wish to thank my W. W. Norton editor, Jill Bialosky, and her assistant, Rebecca Schultz. And thanks to Saskia Hamilton at Barnard College.

Thanks to the Vermont Studio Center and the University of Massachusetts at Lowell for generous support that enabled me to complete this book.

I am deeply indebted to my teachers: thanks always for your instruction and example.

To my colleagues, friends, and dear family, my heartfelt gratitude for your love, friendship, patience, and encouragement.

CPSIA information can be obtained
at www.ICGtesting.com
Printed in the USA
BVHW080901230721
612646BV00008B/707